THE MAN SAW JESUS

WILLIE ECKFORD

WESTBOW
PRESS®
A DIVISION OF THOMAS NELSON
& ZONDERVAN

WestBow Press books may be ordered through booksellers or by contacting:

WestBow Press
A Division of Thomas Nelson & Zondervan
1663 Liberty Drive
Bloomington, IN 47403
www.westbowpress.com
1 (866) 928-1240

ISBN: 978-1-5127-3455-3 (sc)
ISBN: 978-1-5127-3454-6 (e)

Library of Congress Control Number: 2016904230

Print information available on the last page.

WestBow Press rev. date: 04/05/2016

This is my life's testimony. When I was about five years old, things started happening to me that I didn't understand. Now I do, and I want to share my testimony with the world.

One day I woke up late. I tried to get the sheet off me, but it was stuck. I hollered and screamed for my sisters and brothers. I could hear them outside, but they couldn't hear me. I lay there, fighting to get the sheets off. I was sure I was going to die.

About five seconds later, the sheet just opened up. I didn't see anyone, so I jumped out of bed and went outdoors, crying and hollering. My sisters were on the porch. One of them asked me, "What's wrong with you?"

"Something pinned me under the sheet, and I couldn't get out."

My other sister said, "You were probably dreaming. Sit down so we can wash your face. Get some fresh air." I got some fresh air, and everything was okay.

A year later, we moved into town, to a house on Government Street, Pensacola, Florida. As I got older, I started noticing how my dad drank alcohol all the time.

When I was nine, we moved to another house. My brother and I put together an old bicycle for me. My sister and I decided to go for a bike ride one day. She told me to ride on the handlebars. We rode two blocks and then stopped to wait for cars to pass. A blue car came around the corner very fast. There were about six men in the car. The car came straight toward us and ran us over. We fell down, but they kept going. They lost control of the car and hit a tree. They backed the car up and took off again. That's when we ran home. We told my mom and dad what had happened. They asked if we were we hurt, and we said no.

My other sisters and brothers went out to look for the car while Mom called the police. The police came to the house and asked us what happened, and we told them. The police told my mom it would be hard to find them because they didn't have a tag number for the car.

As hard as we got hit, we didn't have to go to the hospital. We were shook up, but there were no broken bones. But my bike was destroyed. God's angels had been around us.

About a week later, Mom said to my dad, "Our children were almost killed last week, and you still drink and act like a fool."

I didn't grow up in a Christian home. My daddy was an alcoholic. As I grew up, Dad's drinking got worse, and he made things really hard for us. I started hating school because of him. The only time there was peace in the house was Monday through Thursday because that was the only time he was sober. Friday through Sunday he was drunk, so we had to stay outdoors until he sobered up, which was sometimes late. We couldn't come in the house because my mother was afraid he would hurt one of us. I would have gone to the authorities, but I was too scared.

When I was about thirteen, I began to hate school because I couldn't get any peace and rest at home because of my dad. I started staying at home, getting into trouble. I was sent to a juvenile detention center. They sent me to a place for teenage boys in another part of Florida. I did my time and got out around the same time public school was out in Pensacola.

Even though I hadn't been attending public school, I received a letter saying I had a summer job. It was a blessing, because if you didn't attend public school, you didn't get a summer job. So I went to work, and everything was going well on the job. But down the road, I lost my job. I went home and told my family what had happened. They were shocked and couldn't believe it. At first I was sad, but then I got mad; I had done nothing wrong. I liked the job and really needed the money because we were poor and couldn't afford school supplies and clothing.

I started getting into trouble again after I lost my job. I began to steal and stay out late, and I ended up going back to detention for over seven months. A visiting teacher came to enroll me in school after I got out. I really wanted to go back to school but couldn't. We tried two schools, but I couldn't get into either of them because I lived outside their districts. So I didn't attend school that year.

Again I got a letter saying I had a summer job. That was another blessing because I hadn't gone to public school that year. This job was at a day care center. I kept that job for the whole summer.

Even though things were going great on the job, life was very bad at home. I got in trouble and went to detention again. While I was in detention this time, one of the workers became attached to me. He told me I deserved a better life, and he said there were people who adopted children. He said he would talk to the judge about it.

He got in touch with my parents to let them know what he was going to do and to see how they felt about it. He told me about a family that wanted to adopt me. I didn't want to leave my family, so I said no. I got out of detention and went back home.

My mom said she was going to leave my dad when I turned sixteen, but she ended up leaving him before then because she could no longer take his abuse. My brothers and I were the only ones left in the house with my dad. Things got worse. The utilities were cut off, and there was no food.

Then my dad stopped drinking and told us to tell Mom he would straighten up and move into another apartment. And he did. One of my brothers discovered where Mom was living. He told her what Dad had said, and she came back home.

Everything went well that first week. The second weekend, my brother and I went out for a while. When we returned home, everything still seemed to be going well. We didn't know, however, that Dad had been arguing with Mom. On Sunday she told us what had happened. My mom said, "Your dad hasn't changed. We got into an argument." She told us she was leaving Monday morning after Dad went to work, and she was never coming back.

On Monday, my brother and I left for a while, and when we got back, she was gone. Dad came home from work and asked us where she was. We told him we didn't know; she had been gone when we got home. He didn't worry about it during the whole week because he knew what he'd done.

When he came home from work, he was already drunk. We heard him from a block away, hollering and using profanity. My brothers and I ran through the kitchen, climbed out the window, and ran downstairs. We stayed away all day long and came home late that night. My dad was asleep by then, but he always kept the door unlocked, so we were able to get in without waking him.

My brother and I got some rest on Saturday because Dad was sober, and everything was going well. He went to the store and bought groceries. Later that night and on Sunday, he got drunk again. So we left again. We took blankets with us because we knew it was going to be a long weekend.

As we walked around the neighborhood, it started raining, and we had nowhere to sleep. We went into a tin shed to get out of the rain. My brother said we would stay there until daybreak, and we would get up before anyone came. Later I felt something wet on my back and woke up to find the shed had flooded. I woke my brother. We went home and slept in the hallway of the apartment building.

The next day we went to live with one of our sisters. We stayed there for a while, and then my aunt came from Mobile and said we could stay with her. She found my brother a job, as he was sixteen, and everything was going great. Sometimes on payday he bought me clothes and shoes.

We stayed at my aunt's house for about a year, and then we moved back to my sister's house in Pensacola. My brother ended up getting in trouble and had to leave for a while. I started staying out late and drinking alcohol. Other family members moved in, and there wasn't enough room for all of us. I moved to my other sister's house. I stayed there for a while, and then my sister moved.

I moved to another sister's house. This sister liked to go out to clubs, and I did too. We worked out a schedule, and when it was her turn to go out, I babysat her three kids.

One night I was leaving the club, and I was really drunk. I took the back street, walking down the railroad tracks. I was so tired I went to sleep on the tracks. My head was on one track, my legs were on the other track, and my body was in the middle. I was so drunk and tired, I thought I could just lie down and go to sleep for a little while and wake up when I heard the train horn. When the horn sounded, I knew I had better get off the tracks, so I got up and staggered and fell in the woods. I stayed there until daybreak because I was too drunk to go any farther.

When daylight came, I got up and staggered home because I was still drunk and tired. I made it home, knocked on the door, and my sister opened it. She asked me where I had been all night. I told her I had been too drunk to come home and had slept outdoors. I had thorns all over me, so I went into the bathroom and checked my body for bruises and scratches from sleeping in the woods. I slept for three or four days to get my strength back.

Two single ladies moved into a house on the corner. They had teenagers around my age, and I got to know them.

My sister asked me to babysit while she went to take care of some business. I started cooking breakfast at about ten in the morning. The front door was open, and I went to close it so the baby wouldn't get out. I went to the door. My right hand was on the knob, and my left was on the window. When I closed the door, my left hand went through the window. The glass broke and split my wrist open. I grabbed my wrist, opened the door, and ran outside. I knew the cut was serious. I was on the porch and moved my hand to look at the cut. Blood shot out everywhere, so I started hollering and took off running. I felt as if the world was on fire. I hollered, "God, please save me! I'm in agony!" I fell on the ground because I couldn't do anything else. I said in my mind, *I've got to get up!* So I was able to get up and run to my neighbors' house on the corner, and they were on the porch.

They saw me and started hollering, "What happened to you?" I told them what happened to my wrist. They told me to come on the porch and told one of their daughters to go get some ice and a rag to treat the cut until the ambulance got there. When I moved my hand for them to wrap it, it felt as if my whole hand was going to fall off. After they wrapped it, I told them to go get my niece from the house and make sure the stove was off.

The ambulance pulled up, and the paramedics came onto the porch. They asked what had happened, and my neighbor told them that I had cut my wrist. They took me in the ambulance to the hospital. When we got there, they took me into a room, and they stuck a long needle in my wrist to deaden it. I was screaming and crying because it hurt so badly. Then they took me to surgery right away. I remember saying to the nurse, "Do not cut my hand off! I'm only sixteen!" And she said, "We're going to try to save it."

After surgery, I woke up in the recovery room. My hand was lying on a pillow, and I turned my head very slowly to look at it because I was nervous. I saw my fingers, and I was a very happy young man!

Several days later the doctors sent a psychiatrist in to ask me questions about the incident. They asked me questions like, "Willie, have you always wanted to hurt yourself?" They thought that I had cut my wrist on purpose. I kept telling them it had been an accident and explained to them what had happened. I kept my word because I was telling the truth. They stopped coming after a few days.

After I got out of the hospital, I went to live with another family member because I didn't want to go back to where I had my accident. I stayed there for a couple of months before I went back home. My health was getting better and better, and things were going well. Eventually we moved to another apartment close to more family. My sister's ways started changing. She was a little help to me. I began to hang with my friends just to get away. Then we started getting into trouble. My oldest sister and her kids were going to move to New York, and she wanted my older brother and me to move with her. So we went, but I didn't like it, and another family member who was there got me a bus ticket back home.

When I got back in town, I no longer had a room at my sister's house because my mom had moved in. I became friends with the neighbor of one of my friends. I started living with him. He was nice man, and we got along well. A few months later, my mom moved out, so I moved back in with my sister. I stayed with my sister for about three years. One of my friends got me a job. I started working at a restaurant in the kitchen. Things were going well; I had income coming in.

While I was taking the bus to work. I met a young woman, and we started dating. Things didn't work out. I met a friend and we moved in as roommate's. Everything was going well there, and I kept going to work. Then things began to change on the job. I started working later shifts, and my ride started leaving me behind. Then I began to get very angry. The third time I had to stay late, my ride left me, and I had to walk home. I finally made it home at three in the morning. When I went back to work the next morning, my buddies and I started drinking on our break. They gave us three or four one-hour breaks every day.

After work we would stop at a little club to drink some more because we were not happy about the way they treated us on the job. One night I got really drunk. My buddy and I were wrestling and playing on the highway. All I remember is running behind my friend and waking up at my sister's house in the bathtub. Blood was all over my body. I got out of the tub and looked in the mirror to see what was going on. When I saw my face, I couldn't stand to look at it because I looked like a monster. I went in the bedroom to rest, and my sister knocked on the door and asked me if I was going to be all right. She told me what had happened. My friends had dropped me off at her house the night before.

A couple of weeks went by, and God started healing me. I got on the bus and went back home to my roommate's house. I walked into the yard and knocked on the door, and my roommate opened it. She looked at me as if to say "What happened?" and I told her that I got drunk, fell, and skinned my face. She didn't believe me. She started fussing, and I didn't want to hear it. I was tired and went to sleep.

I got up on Monday morning and went to work. I worked all the way to Friday night. I had a lot of work to do that night, and my ride couldn't wait any longer, so he left. I finally finished my work. I had to walk home again. I finally made it home, tired and worn out. I told my roommate that I got fired from my job, and she got very angry. She told me that she had a friend who could get me another job.

I worked for about a year in a new job and began to get interested in a different type of work. I didn't care anymore, so I ended up getting fired. I told my roommate I was moving out. My oldest sister moved back into town, so I moved back in with her. She finally moved into a bigger apartment. I got a job at a restaurant. Then things weren't going well at home, so I left. I still had my job, but I was living on the streets. My boss said that he was opening up another restaurant, and I could get another job working with him.

Within two weeks I moved into a room and began working at my new job. I was happy in my own place! I started drinking again and hanging out late at night. I said to myself that I needed to stop drinking, and I started watching Christian programs on TV. Things got a lot better for me. My mom finally got over my dad and moved into her own house. I visited her a lot, but she wanted me to move in with her. I told my landlord that I was moving out, and he was sad because he didn't want me to leave. I left and moved in with my mom. When I moved in, I started drinking again, and she was very angry about it. She told me not to be like my daddy.

Eventually I stopped drinking. One of my nieces moved in with us. She was going to church a lot, and I told her that one Sunday I wanted to go to church with her. She called the pastor and told her that her uncle wanted to visit the church. When I went, I liked the service and the church members.

The restaurant that I had been working for went out of business, but I kept going to church. Every Wednesday and Thursday night I was there for prayer meetings and Bible study. God blessed me with another job.

Rumors started going around about the pastor. She got discouraged and left the church. She told me to stay in church no matter what. She told one of the deacons in the church to make sure to pick me up every Sunday, Wednesday, and Thursday, and not to let me stop going to church. I went on two Sundays. He came to pick me up for prayer and Bible study on Wednesday and Thursday, but I didn't go. He realized then that I didn't want to go, so he stopped coming.

I decided to move out of my mom's house. My mom was happy that I was doing something for myself. She said I was a grown man, and I needed to be on my own. One day when I was going to work, I saw a house for rent, so I wrote the phone number down and I got in touch with the landlady. She told me to meet her so she could show me the house. I liked the house, and she told me the amount of the deposit and how the much the rent would be. I moved in the next month.

I was enjoying living in my house by myself. I was going to work, and everything was going well. Around Christmas, there was a Christmas party at my job, and I drank a lot of alcohol. Someone had to take me home; I was drunk and sick. That Monday morning I went back to work still feeling kind of sick from the party, but I made it through the day. I made it home that night from work, and some coworkers stopped by and wanted to drink some more alcohol, so I joined in.

Not too long after that night, I made up my mind to stop drinking for a while. I started watching Christian television again. When I got off work one night, I was real tired, so I went to bed early. I woke up around three o'clock the next morning. I was lying on my mattress on the floor in the living room by the window. I heard a sound like a missile coming toward me. It hit my forehead, went through my head, and came out the back. I felt as if my head had exploded. I was hollering, screaming, and praying in my mind because I couldn't get the words out of my mouth. I felt something grab me and pull me through the wall; I saw my upper body lying on the porch, and my legs and feet were still in the house. I was still calling on Jesus to save me because I knew I was going to Hades.

Within seconds, my upper body went back into the house. I got up, walked to the door, and went outside. I ran to the corner. My heart was beating very fast. I was nervous, and my whole body broke out in a sweat. I said to myself, *What just happened to me?* I was so terrified, I didn't want to go back to my house, but I knew I had to get some rest because I had to go to work later that day. So I walked back to the house and sat in my chair on the porch. I was scared to go back into the house, so I sat there for about twenty-five minutes and drifted in and out of sleep. I knew I had to go back in and get some real sleep.

I finally went back into the house and got my Bible. I lay down and put the Bible on my chest. I thought to myself, *Satan, if you want me, you're going to have to come through Jesus to get me.* I fell asleep and woke up around six in the morning. I went in the bathroom and looked in the mirror that hung on my bathroom door. I was checking to see if all my limbs were still attached to me! After that I went to work and told one of my coworkers what had happened. He said it was the devil trying to kill me. I didn't think about it anymore and just went on with my life.

I kept sinning when I should have repented. I decided to move out of the house I was living in. I got in touch with one of my cousins, and she helped me move things. I moved a block away to some apartments. Everything went well for several years until the company I had been working for—for ten years—closed down. The boss told the workers that, if we wanted another job, he knew someone who could help us. He told us to be at a certain place early on Monday morning, and only two of us showed up. We met the man who would help us, and he asked us what type of job we were looking for. I said I was looking for a job in another restaurant. He told me there was a job at a restaurant two blocks away. He told me to meet him there Tuesday morning at nine.

I showed up, and he introduced me to the boss. I told him I needed a day job. The man who got me the new job gave me some money and told me to take two weeks off to rest. When my two weeks were up, I started working and got to know the people there. It was a good job. It was a morning job, and I liked it so much.

One day when I was at work doing my prep work for the pizza, a sharp pain hit me in my midsection. It felt as if someone had stuck me with a sharp object. Even though it hurt, I kept on working, made it through that day, and went home. For three days in a row I had the same pain on the job. On my day off, I got up, took a bath, and went into the bedroom to put my clothes on. I looked in the mirror and saw a big knot protruding from my midsection. I said to myself, *What's going on now?* I got dressed, ignored the knot, and went out and enjoyed my off day. I made it home safely.

The next morning when I woke up, the knot was gone and I went on to work. I told one of my coworkers who worked with me in the back that I was having pain in my midsection. He said, "You need to go get that checked because I had the same thing and found out that I had a hernia in my intestines." I said "We'll see." I really didn't want to go to the hospital. I finished my work and went on home.

When I got home that day, the knot appeared again. I was in severe pain for at least seven hours. I rode my bike to my cousin's house and asked her if she could take me to the hospital. She said, "Yeah, come on. Let's go." We made it to the hospital. As I walked to the counter to sign in, I was hollering because I was in so much pain. My cousin signed me in, and they told us to have a seat because four or five people were in front of us. I went to the back of the lobby screaming and hollering, rolling around on the floor, holding my midsection. My cousin came back there to pray for me. She said, "Lord, please stop the pain." They finally called my name and took me into an exam room to get my blood pressure. I said to the woman, "No time to take my blood pressure. I'm in too much pain." So they took me to another room, and about a minute later the doctor came in to see me. He asked me what the problem was, and I told him. He said, "Let me take a look at it." He asked me, "How long has it been like this?" I told him over a week. He said I could have caught gangrene and died. Then he pushed down on the knot, which was my intestines, and they went back in. He told me to keep my hand on the spot so they wouldn't come back out. He said that they were going to do surgery in the morning. They were going to cut me on both the right and left side of my stomach and put a camera through my navel.

The next morning I went into surgery. When I got there I was very nervous because I saw all the different tools. The nurse told me to relax, that everything was going to be all right. She said they were going to put me to sleep. She told me to count to ten. I started counting, and that's all I remember because I went to sleep.

When I woke up later that night, the nurse was there. I told her that I had to have surgery in the morning. She told me that I had already had surgery; I just didn't remember because I'd been sleep. She rolled me on my bed into a recovery room, and later some of my family came to see me.

The next day my sister bought me the pictures from my surgery. After the visiting hours were over, the doctor came to check on me. He said that the surgery went well. He told me that he would keep me one more day for observation. He told me that, when I went home, I should drink a lot of fluid, not pick up anything over five pounds, and take some time off from work. I did what he told me to do.

After about three weeks, I went back to work and was able to work my full schedule. Then Christmas came. I was thinking that it would be nice to get the family together at the park by the water for the holiday. So I started making phone calls to get everyone together. I told them to meet up at the park on Saturday at two in the afternoon. Saturday rolled around, and I was the first one there, so I waited for everyone else to get there. At around 2:30, everyone started to show up. I was really pleased that everyone showed up because we really hadn't had a family reunion in a while.

Time flew by so fast because everyone was having a good time. At around nine in the evening, people started to leave. A couple of people asked me if I wanted a ride because I had been drinking a lot. I told them that I would be all right. I would just ride my bike home. When the last person pulled out of the parking lot, I left. I made it home safely. I went into the house and sat down for a little bit, and I got bored. I decided to get on my bike and go for a ride to get some fresh air because I didn't want to go to bed feeling drunk.

To be safe, I rode on the back street away from cars. All I can remember is waking up in the ambulance. They told me that I had fallen off my bike and landed on my face. They told me that they were taking me to the hospital. When we got to the hospital, they rolled me into a room, and about six doctors and nurses came in. They examined me, and one doctor told me that my face was swollen and scarred up real bad, and they might have to do plastic surgery. They checked my right eye and told me that they might have to take it out. I began to say to myself, *Lord, don't let this happen.*

The doctors and nurses left the room. About a minute later, one nurse came back in and told me the doctor said that they were going to let me go after a couple hours. She told me to wash my face every day with soap and warm water, and she would get my prescription for the swelling. She said that, if the swelling didn't go down within a week, I should come back to the emergency room. I asked her if she had a mirror so I could see my face. She asked me was I sure, because I was bruised up pretty badly. I told her yes, and she got the mirror. When I saw my face, I couldn't believe it. It looked bad.

They put me in a wheelchair, rolled me to the front of the building, and called me a cab. On the way home, the cab driver asked me what had happened to me. He asked me if I had been robbed. I told him that I had fallen off my bike, and he couldn't believe it. I made it home, went into the house, and lay on my bed.

The next morning I got up and did what the doctor told me to do. I called my boss and told him that there had been something slippery on the street, and I had lost control of my bike. I lied because I didn't want him to know that I had been drunk. He told me that he would come over the next day to take me to get my prescription filled. He came, and we went to the pharmacy. When I got back home, I washed my face again and took some medicine.

About five days later, I began to see scabs come up on my face, and the swelling was going down. The next week when

I was washing my face, the scabs started coming off. That third week I was able to go back to work. God had healed me so fast.

I was working and living in Florida, where there are lots of hurricanes. The day before Hurricane Ivan hit, one of my family members came to get me. This storm destroyed the apartment complex that I was living in. The owner gave us time to move out. I made my way around to see what had happened to my job. The roof had been damaged, and the building had been condemned.

Things started getting better, and my friend helped me financially. My neighbor got me a job with him. I didn't like the job because there were a lot of disrespectful coworkers. I worked for a month and then quit. I saw my neighbor, and he was angry with me for quitting. I decided to find a job on my own. I walked around an area where there were several restaurants, and I saw a sign announcing that a restaurant would be opening soon. I knocked on the door, and a man let me in. I explained to him that I was looking for a day job working in the kitchen. He told me that the day job was mine. I filled out the application, and he told me to come back the next week for orientation.

The next week I started working. Now that I had a job, I started looking for an apartment. I found one and called to get information. The landlord told me about the deposit and rent, and I moved in. I stayed there over a year and then left because each month the rent got higher. About a month later, I moved into another apartment in the neighborhood. Meanwhile, several men at my job left, saying they were moving back home out of town. One man remained, and things started going downhill. Finally, I left too.

I got in touch with my friend and told him what was going on. He said he knew a restaurant that would never close down, and he gave me a man's name and told me to get in contact with him. I did, and I started working the next day. Within that first year on the job, I started having chest pains and dizziness. I noticed that my health was breaking down. I told one of my coworkers that I might have to stop working. It was hard, but I made it through that year.

One day I was leaving work on my bicycle, and the bike started shaking as if it was possessed. Before I knew it, I was flying in the air. Just as I saw a police car, I landed on the right side of my body and skinned my arm. The police officer got out of his car and told me not to move. He said that he had seen everything, and he would call the ambulance. The ambulance came, and paramedics asked me if I was I badly hurt. They were going to take me to the hospital. They helped me up, and we got into the ambulance. I asked the police officer not to leave my bicycle because it was brand new. He said he would bring it to the hospital.

They took me to the hospital and treated my arm. The doctor told me that it wasn't broken, just bruised pretty badly. I had to stay for observation before they would let me go home. I stayed for about two hours, and then they released me. I was able to ride my bike home with one arm. I made it home and called my employer to let him know what had happen and that I needed some time off.

I stayed off work for about two months because of my injury. I went back to work around the Christmas holidays and worked through the end of January 2009. It was close to payday, and I said to myself, *I get paid on February 8.* I worked on Sunday and was off on Monday and Tuesday. I got paid every Monday. During the whole day at work on Sunday, I was feeling weak. I went home, and I started feeling weaker. I said to myself, *On Monday I will go to the job, get my check, and then come back home.*

I went to bed early on Sunday night. The next morning I went to the job to get my check, but I didn't cash it because I wasn't feeling good. I just went back home. On Tuesday morning, I woke up very early, at around six. I drank a cup of coffee then lay back down. When I woke up again it was 9:00. I was lying on my back, and the room started spinning. I jumped up from the bed and I said "Help me, Jesus" about three times. I made it through the den and was almost to the kitchen when I was thrown back toward the bathroom. I was holding on to the wall to keep from hurting myself. I got enough strength to make it back through the den. I was trying to make it to the front door, but I kept falling. So I tried to crawl, but I kept flipping over like a baby.

I just gave up and started repenting. I asked God to forgive me for all my sins. And I said "If it's your will for me to go home, I'm ready. There's nothing else I can do. I can't get up." I was lying on the floor, and when I looked up I could see my love seat. I saw someone—or something—that looked like a demon. It said to me, "I have waited a long time for you!"

I ignored it and felt a presence behind me. I tried to look behind me, but all I saw was a shadow. I could feel the presence of the Lord. I still couldn't get up, but after a few seconds went by, I was able to get up. I walked to the sofa and put my clothes on. I was right by the kitchen and tried to run through, but I was thrown back again. It felt as if a tornado had come into the house, because I was spinning around and around. I didn't give up. I kept trying to get out of the house.

I finally made it into the kitchen. I had a small kitchen with a big glass table. I was crawling past the table and then, all of sudden, I was slammed into the iron table legs. It hurt so much, I said, "God, I broke my neck!" I had my hand on my neck, and I felt someone looking at me. I turned toward the sink, and in the corner I saw Jesus.

The first thing that came to my mind was, *That's the son of the living God, Jesus Christ, in my house!* He was looking at me, and I was looking at him. I wanted to say something, but I couldn't get my mouth to open.

I held my head down for a moment because I felt unworthy. When I looked back up, he was gone. I had been blessed to see him, and I was amazed. I made it to the living room and managed to get onto the big leather sofa. I lay back and said to myself, *I can't go any further. I have got to rest.* Suddenly the sofa flipped over on top of me. I was hollering and screaming, "God, get this sofa off me!" I was finally able to get the sofa righted. I lay on it again. I thought to myself, *This sofa weighs at least two hundred eighty pounds, and I weigh a hundred twenty pounds. There's no way I could have flipped this sofa onto myself!* I rolled off the sofa and landed on the floor by the door. I had enough strength to pull myself up and grab the doorknob. I opened the screen door and looked to my right. I saw my neighbor sitting on the porch. I called to him, and he answered me. I said, "Will you do me a favor?" He said, "Yes." I asked him if he would give me a ride to the hospital, and he said he would.

When I staggered over to him, he asked me which hospital I wanted to go to. I said, "Any one. I don't care. Just get me to a hospital." When we got there, he went inside to get a wheelchair because I couldn't walk. He wheeled me in and signed me in. He told the nurse, "I brought my neighbor in because he was dizzy, and I don't know what's wrong with him." They took my blood pressure, and then took me to a back examination room. A couple minutes later my neighbor came back there with me.

I had no control over my body. My arms and legs were going up and down. My neighbor got a nurse and told her what was happening. Another nurse came and gave me a shot to calm me down. A few minutes later, I had to use the restroom. My neighbor had to help me, but when I got there, I couldn't use it. He helped me about twelve times, but each time I still couldn't use it. So he decided to go get the nurse and let them know what was going on again. When the nurse came in, he told me that they were going to put a catheter in. And they did. I felt a lot better. I ended up going to sleep.

When I woke up, my neighbor and sister walked in the room. She asked me what was wrong and asked if I had been drinking. I shook my head and went back to sleep. When I woke up again, it was about 10:30 at night. I was feeling good. One of the nurses walked in and said, "How you feeling now?" I said, "I feel a lot better." He asked me if I felt able to go home, and I said yes. He asked me if I wanted them to call a family member to come get me, or if I wanted a cab. I told him a cab. He called the cab and came back to get me. He put me in a wheelchair and wheeled me outdoors to wait for the cab. The cab came, and the nurse helped me get inside.

The cab took me home. When I got out of the cab, I started walking in the yard. I started falling. I said out loud, "Not again! I just left the hospital!"

I looked over to my neighbor's house and saw his car parked in the yard. I wanted to go over there, but I didn't because another thought came to my mind telling me to go into the house and go to sleep, just as I had done at the hospital. On the way to the door, I kept falling down. I made it onto the porch and got my key in the door, thank God. When I got inside, I went to my bedroom in the back of the house. I lay on the bed and tried to get some sleep. I was in severe pain. I felt as if someone was beating my head with a baseball bat. I said, "God!" I got out of the bed and staggered to the front door. I managed to open the door and get myself onto the porch. I fell down. I saw one of my other neighbors, but he couldn't see me, and I couldn't talk.

I crawled into the yard and stopped for a moment. I couldn't figure out what to do. I was confused. I said to myself, *Maybe if I crawl into the middle of the street, someone will see me when they drive by.* I decided not to go into the street. So I turned and crawled backwards to my neighbor's house. I crawled up the steps and had enough strength to hit the screen door. After that I just lay on my back. He came to the door and looked. He didn't see me, but I saw him. Then he looked down and saw me. He told me to hold on so he could turn the stove off because he had been in the kitchen. Then he returned with a blanket.

He wrapped me up and helped me to the car, and he drove me back to the hospital. He went inside to get a wheelchair. Then he came back and wheeled me in. He went to the front desk and told the nurses that I had just left about thirty minutes before, and something was seriously wrong with me. The nurse said, "The hospital is full of people. He can't skip ahead in line." My neighbor wheeled me to the middle of the floor and told me that he would be right back; he had to move his car. I was in so much pain, and I fell out of the wheelchair. I was knocked unconscious, and when I woke up I saw nurses. They said that they had to get me on the bed to get my blood pressure. Then they got me out of the bed, put me back into the wheelchair, and took my blood pressure. After that the nurse started to wheel me to my room, but we didn't make it. The wheelchair flipped over, and I flew in the air.

I saw my nurse fall back and hit her head on the wall. She fell down to the floor. She was hollering, "Help me! Help me!" The other nurses came and helped me up. They put me back into the wheelchair and wheeled me into a room and strapped me down. I went to sleep, and when I woke up it was about seven in the morning. The nurse walked in and said to me, "We have a room for you, and now we can start treating you."

They took me to my room and later started bringing me medicine. The doctor came in and explained to me that I'd had a stroke on the left side of my brain. First they put an IV in my arm, and then they hooked me up to a heart monitor. They also put a catheter in me and gave me leg warmers to loosen up the blood that was clogged in my veins. They were constantly checking my blood. One of my family members who worked there walked in and gave me an electrocardiogram and told me that she would tell the rest of the family what was going on.

So she got in touch with my family, and they came. Two of my family members anointed me with oil and started to pray for me. They were saying things like "It's going to be all right" and "You're going to get well soon." Later on, my family members left. The nurses started me on therapy. They wheeled me around so I could get used to seeing people. They said, "Soon you're going to have to go home and be around people and go on with your life." When I got back to my room they told me that they would do the same thing tomorrow after breakfast.

My roommate was agitating me because he kept the TV real loud, so he had to leave and be relocated to another room. Every day my appetite increased, and I was getting stronger. As the weeks went by, one of the nurses started getting attached to me. She told me that she worried about me when she was at home. She said she had never felt that way about a patient. She also said, "There's something special about that man."

Before she left, the nurse would look at me from the hall for about ten seconds. She really was a nice nurse.

I had to do a little more therapy before I left. One of the nurses came in and told me that the doctor would let me go home in two or three days. The day I was released, one of my family members came and got me and took me home. I was at home alone for about an hour until the rest of the family came over. They brought me water and food and said that, starting the next day, they were going to have to take care of all my personal business, starting with outpatient therapy.

I went to therapy every Wednesday for five weeks. After I finished my therapy, I was able to get around better. I started walking in my neighborhood with my cane, going places I used to go. People recognized me from before I had my stroke, and I started witnessing to them. They were saying things like "I'm so glad you shared your testimony with me" and "I needed to hear this because you bring me hope." I started riding the bus and witnessed to more people. Certain people asked me if I could come to their church to talk to the young people because they needed to hear this. I didn't go because God spoke to me and told me it wasn't time and that I needed to write a book first. After I while, I realized that I needed to move out of my house.

Eventually I was able to ride my bike again, so I rode to the west side of town to look for an apartment. I found an apartment and made an appointment to meet the owner to look inside. I called a family member to come with me to meet the owner. When I looked inside I didn't like what I saw, but the landlord told me that he had more apartments on my side of town. So we followed him to go look at the other apartments. We went into one, and I walked through. I liked what I saw. I told him that I would pay my deposit, and I moved in a month later. I've been here ever since. When I moved in, there were quite a few ungodly people here, but now they no longer live here. I used to see my neighbor. One day I asked him what church he went to, and he told me. I told him maybe I would go with him the following Sunday. I went on Sunday and joined the same day.

I continued to witness and kept going on with my life. One night I was awakened by something trying to pull me out of my bed. I kicked at it trying to get it to stop. Eventually it stopped pulling. I got out of the bed and said, "Satan, that's not going to work!"

Months later, on September 1, 2012, I was watching TV, but I was tired so I decided to go to bed early at around eight o'clock. I went to sleep and woke up about a half hour later. I was just lying in the bed and I heard a loud sound. It sounded like an airplane flying across the apartment building. All of a sudden it felt as if the plane landed on me. I saw my soul leave my body. I was trying to get up, but I couldn't, and I was crying and screaming, "Help me, God! Save me! My soul is going to Hades!" I could see my soul falling down a tunnel, and I knew I was going to Hades. I felt the heat, and I saw the fire. Then suddenly my soul came back to my body. I got up and walked into the living room. My body was shaking. The first thing that came to my mind was, *Satan tried to steal my soul; he thought I was sleep, but I wasn't.*

"That if thou shalt confess with thy mouth the Lord Jesus, and shalt believe in thine heart that God hath raised him from the dead, thou shalt be saved" (Romans 10:9 King James Version).

Amen, God Bless!

About the Author

My Name is Willie Eckford I was born in Pensacola Florida.

I came from a small family we didnt have much but made a

way. People always said i was a nice day.

Printed in the United States
By Bookmasters